# DK Eye Wonder
# Weather

LONDON, NEW YORK, MUNICH,
MELBOURNE, and DELHI

**Written and edited by** Lorrie Mack
**Designed by** Cheryl Telfer
and Helen Chapman

**Publishing manager** Sue Leonard
**Managing art editor** Clare Shedden
**Jacket design** Chris Drew
**Picture researcher** Sarah Stewart-Richardson
**Production** Shivani Pandey
**DTP designer** Almudena Díaz
**DTP assistant** Pilar Morales
**Consultant** Ben Morgan

First American Edition, 2004
Published in the United States by
DK Publishing, Inc.
375 Hudson Street
New York, New York 10014

04 05 06 07 08 10 9 8 7 6 5 4 3 2 1

A Cataloging-in-Publication record for this book is
available from the Library of Congress.

ISBN 0-7566-0323-4

Color reproduction by Colourscan, Singapore
Printed and bound in Italy by L.E.G.O.

Discover more at
**www.dk.com**

# Contents

# What's weather?

"Weather" is what the sky and the air outside are like—cloudy, snowy, sunny, or windy. A wide band of air—the atmosphere—surrounds Earth, but weather only happens near the ground, below the cloud tops. This area is called the cloud layer or troposphere.

Satellite

Spacecraft

Meteor trails

Aurora (polar lights)

Outer space

Thermosphere

Mesosphere

Stratosphere

Troposphere

## Weather facts

● Together, energy from the Sun and moisture in the air create our weather.

● The air has lots of moisture in it because water covers 75 percent of Earth's surface.

● Weather kills more people than any other other natural force on the planet.

## Thin skin
If the Earth were a huge apple, the whole atmosphere would be thinner than the skin. Driving straight through all its layers in a car, you would reach outer space in about three hours.

*The clouds that constantly swirl around Earth are clearly visible from weather satellites in space.*

*All our weather goes on in the layer of the atmosphere closest to Earth—the troposphere.*

## Out of this world

Above the troposphere is the stratosphere. Here, because the air is very dry, there is no rain or wind. Pilots like to fly at this level because they can be sure of a smooth ride.

*When an airplane flies above the clouds, the passengers have a magical view from the windows.*

Every day, we live with one of the most powerful natural forces of all— our weather.

sun

wind

frost

rain

snow

# The seasons

When one part of the world is basking in summer, another part is shivering in winter. This happens because Earth, which leans to one side, travels on a long journey around the Sun.

## On the tilt

Earth is a round ball with an imaginary stick, or axis, running through the center (dotted red line). This axis is tilted so one half of Earth gets more sunlight than the other at any one time, and is therefore sunnier.

## March

It's spring in the northern hemisphere, and fall at the other end of the world.

SPRING

FALL

## Ball of fire

The Sun is a fiery star made of burning gas. We depend on it for light, heat, and energy. Without the Sun, there would be no life on Earth.

Axis

Equator

SUMMER

WINTER

## North and south

The equator is an imaginary ring around Earth's middle (yellow line). The area above it is called the northern hemisphere, while the area below it is the southern hemisphere.

## June

The northern hemisphere is tilted toward the Sun, so the people there are enjoying summer. South of the equator, there is much less sun, so winter is setting in.

A year has 365 days because Earth

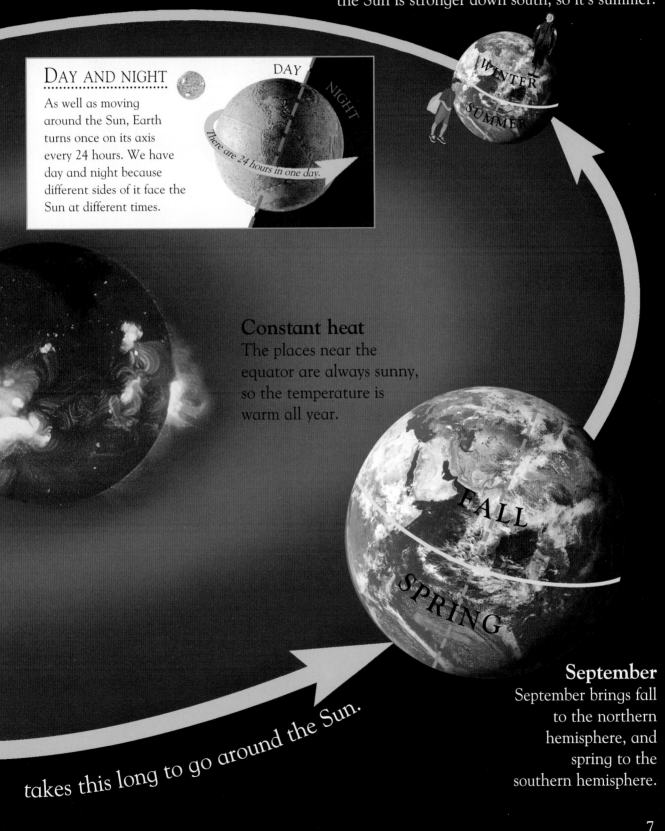

## December

In December, the northern hemisphere leans away from the Sun, so it's winter there. But the Sun is stronger down south, so it's summer.

### DAY AND NIGHT

As well as moving around the Sun, Earth turns once on its axis every 24 hours. We have day and night because different sides of it face the Sun at different times.

DAY

NIGHT

There are 24 hours in one day.

WINTER

SUMMER

### Constant heat

The places near the equator are always sunny, so the temperature is warm all year.

FALL

SPRING

## September

September brings fall to the northern hemisphere, and spring to the southern hemisphere.

takes this long to go around the Sun.

7

# The power of the Sun

Earth is constantly bombarded with rays from the Sun—a huge ball of burning gases in space. As well as producing heat and light, the Sun controls Earth's weather.

## Warmth and water
Heat from the Sun turns the moisture from leafy trees and plants into invisible water vapor in the air. The same thing happens with the water in lakes and oceans.

*Water sometimes disappears into the air and becomes water vapor. This process is called evaporation.*

## Clouds
Moisture hovers in the sky in the form of clouds. When the clouds get full, the tiny droplets in them stick together and become drops of rain.

## Wind

The Sun's rays warm pockets of air, which causes them to rise. Cool air then rushes in to fill the gap. This movement of air is what we call wind.

## Rain

Water from clouds falls as rain. If the air is cold enough, the moisture turns into snowflakes instead of raindrops. Whatever form it takes, all moisture that falls to the ground is called precipitation.

## Sunny facts

● If all the Sun's energy could be harnessed for one second, it would power the United States for 9 million years.

● Earth is a tiny dot compared with the Sun, which is big enough to swallow our planet a million times.

## Starting again

Some rain and melted snow flow back into our rivers and oceans. This water is called runoff. Soon it will evaporate into clouds again.

# Clouds in the sky

Clouds are made from drops of water. The amount of water in each cloud, its height, and the air temperature determine what kind it is. There are three main types—stratus, cumulus, and cirrus—and lots of combinations of these.

## Cloudy facts

- In Latin, *stratus* means layer, *cirrus* means hair, and *cumulus* means heap.

- Clouds that have "nimbus" or "nimbo" in their name are rain clouds.

- Clouds that have "alto" in their name form at a medium height.

## Cumulus

These clouds are plump and fluffy like cotton balls. Small white ones appear on clear, sunny days, but cumulus clouds that are big and black (called cumulonimbus) mean rain or snow storms are on the way.

*Stratocumulus clouds have layers as well as the bumpy surface of cumulus clouds. Their soft gray shapes often produce drizzle or light rain.*

## Stratus

Of all the main types, stratus clouds are lowest in the sky. Sometimes they sit right on the ground to form fog. Although stratus means "layer," the layers aren't always clear—often, stratus clouds just make the sky look gray.

*Cirrocumulus clouds are a cross between cirrus and cumulus types. When their regular waves of tiny cloud clumps form a pattern that looks like fish scales, we call this a "mackerel sky."*

## Cirrus

High, wispy, feathery clouds are called cirrus. Here, the air is so cold that clouds are made from ice crystals rather than water drops. Sometimes, strong winds blow them into long strands or "mare's tails" because they look like horse's tails.

## Sky map

Clouds are named according to their height and how they're formed. Even those that look quite similar can have different names at different heights.

Some cumulonimbus clouds are 7 miles (11 km) tall.

Cirrus

Airplane contrail

Cirrostratus

Cirrocumulus

Altostratus

Stratocumulus

Cumulonimbus

Cumulus

Nimbostratus

Stratus

*Against a blue sky, contrails sometimes look like city streets made of clouds.*

# Cloud gallery

There is nothing unusual about cloudy skies—most of us see them all the time. But we might be surprised if the clouds looked like flying saucers, sheets of water, or clusters of colored lights.

## Human-made clouds

When jet planes crisscross the sky, they leave behind long, straight tails of vapor that look like clouds. These are known as contrails.

### Wavy nights

Clouds that appear at night and look like waves on the sea are called noctilucent clouds. The name "noctilucent" comes from the Latin words for "night" and "shine."

## Painted clouds

When sunlight passes through the water droplets or ice crystals in a cloud, it can produce beautiful shimmering colors.

## Bumpy warning

The peculiar rounded shape of these storm clouds gives them their name. They're called mammatus clouds, from "mamma," the Latin word for "breast."

*Mammatus clouds are often a sign that there's a tornado on the way.*

All these bumps are caused by downdrafts of air.

## Flying clouds

Lenticular clouds got their name because they look a little like lenses, but some of them look more like flying saucers!

Saucer-shaped clouds can "hover" for hours.

# Living in a cloud

Sometimes it's so foggy outside, you feel as if you're walking through a cloud. In a way, you are! Fog is actually a cloud that is sitting on the ground instead of floating in the air. There are several different ways fog is made.

*The Golden Gate Bridge in San Francisco is often surrounded by fog.*

Mist and fog are different types of mist is just finer and lighter

## Rolling in

When warm, damp air blows over cold land or a cold ocean current, its moisture turns into fog. This type is called advection fog.

14

## Mountain mist

On wooded hills, moisture given off by trees turns into fog during the night. By dawn, it has settled into the valleys below. Later, when the Sun warms the air, this moisture evaporates, and the fog clears.

the same thing—than fog.

## Poison air

When fog combines with smoke, it forms heavy, smelly air. Years ago, London, England, had fogs so thick—even during the day– that people called them "pea-soupers." Then, smoke came from the dirty coal fires that heated most buildings. Today, similar conditions, known as smog, are caused by pollution from cars and factories.

## Hazy days

When the ground loses (radiates) heat and gets very cold, it cools the air above it, making water vapor condense into fine droplets. This creates the most common type of fog, known as "radiation" fog.

# Rain, rain

Clouds are made of tiny droplets of water. When a cloud takes on more and more moisture, the droplets get bigger. Eventually, they get so heavy that they fall to the ground as drops—small ones are called drizzle, and big, heavy ones are called rain.

## How much rain?

Scientists measure rain in a simple gauge set into the ground. After the drops fall through the funnel at the top, they are collected in the main cylinder below.

### Average yearly rainfall

**Kauai, Hawaii**
460 in (11,680 mm)

**New York**
44.5 in (1,130 mm)

**London, England**
24 in (610 mm)

**Berlin, Germany**
23 in (580 mm)

**Cairo, Egypt**
1 in (25 mm)

**Arica, Chile**
0.03 in (7 mm)

## Falling shapes

Most people think raindrops are shaped like teardrops, but they actually look more like squashed buns.

*New raindrops are round, but they flatten out gradually as they fall.*

## Scary skies

Rain clouds hold a huge amount of water, which makes them so dense that light can't get through. This is why they look dark and scary. The heaviest rain falls from the biggest, blackest clouds.

## Poison rain

When chemicals pour into the air from factories and cars, they react with water vapor to form harmful acids. The result—acid rain—kills forests, poisons water, and even wears away stone.

## Rainy facts

- On the Hawaiian island of Kauai, there are only about 15 days in the year when it doesn't rain.

- Drizzle falls more slowly than rain, since it is much finer. It takes about 700 drizzle drops to make one raindrop.

## Deadly showers

Heavy rain can cause terrible floods that destroy life and property. When storms hit the Zacatenco River in Mexico, its raging waters had enough power to bring this bridge down.

# White skies

When the air is cold, the moisture in clouds freezes into ice crystals without turning into rain first. These crystals stick together and float to the ground as snowflakes.

*There can be as many as 200 ice crystals in one snowflake.*

*In a really bad blizzard, people can hardly see where they're going.*

### Swirling curtain

When snow is coming down thick and fast, we call it a blizzard. Sometimes, even when a blizzard is over, wind whips up the snow on the ground so it seems like it's still falling.

## White lace

Most snowflakes look like lacy, six-pointed stars, but some have very different shapes.

*These flakes are described as stellar, meaning starlike.*

*Snowflakes with six flat sides are called plates.*

*Columns are long, hollow flakes of snow.*

## Cozy snow

The Inuit people of the Arctic build small huts from blocks of snow. These temporary shelters, which they use like tents, are called igloos.

## Look out below!

Layers of snow can build up so high that a slight movement can tip them over. Tumbling, crashing snow like this is called an avalanche.

### Snowy facts

● Snow is so important to the Inuit that they have over 100 words for it, including *piqsig* (blowing snow) and *auviq* (good snow for igloos).

● In April 1921, 6 ft 4 in (1.93 m) of snow fell in 24 hours at Silver Lake, Colorado.

*A big avalanche can bury people and buildings in seconds.*

## Fallen snow looks like a white blanket.

*Fallen snow looks white and sparkly because it reflects nearly all the light that hits it.*

## Cold and dry

The heaviest snows fall when the temperature is just below freezing. Very, very cold places hardly ever get any snow.

# Icy showers

When solid pellets of ice fall
out of the sky, we call it hail.
Some hailstones are about
the size of plums, and
others are smaller
than peas.

*Then it falls, collecting*

*An ice crystal gets caught in an updraft.*

*Giant hailstones
can smash through
roofs, hurt people,
and flatten crops.*

*These hailstones are as big as tennis balls!*

## Birth of a hailstone

Inside huge storm clouds,
strong, freezing winds
whirl around constantly.
Any ice crystals inside
get tossed up and down,
building up more and
more frozen layers on
each crystal. These
layers turn the tiny
crystals into hailstones.

## Icy missiles

Small hailstones are round and white, but
bigger ones usually have knobby shapes and
jagged surfaces. The largest hailstone ever
recorded measured 17 in (43 cm) across.

*The air at the top of a cloud is colder than the air at the bottom.*

Each round trip adds another layer of ice.

moisture on the way. Up it goes again, freezing at the top.

The ice ball keeps getting bigger and bigger

until it falls out of the sky.

### Falling danger
A single huge hailstone shattered this windscreen.

### Road risk
Driving through a hailstorm can be deadly. It's hard to see, the road is slippery, and really big hailstones can damage cars and trucks.

21

# Dew and frost

On cool nights, moisture in the air turns into water as it drops to the ground, covering everything with morning dew. On freezing cold days, it hardens as frost.

### Dawn sparkle

On cool mornings, you will find glittery drops of dew covering every surface. On this delicate spiderweb, the dewdrops look like tiny jewels.

### Nature's glaze

If the temperature falls after the dew has settled, the moisture often freezes into a covering of clear, smooth ice, like on these berries.

### Fern frost

When damp air comes in contact with cold glass, the water vapor turns to ice crystals. These look like fine lace, or the feathery, ferny leaves that give this frost its name.

### Hoar frost

As water vapor in the air touches frozen surfaces, it sometimes forms spiky ice needles instead of a smooth coating. These spikes are called hoar frost.

# Rime frost

During very cold weather, icy winds
create a crusty coating called rime
frost on wet leaves and branches.
Because it forms so quickly, rime
is thick and hard, with a surface
that looks like sugar.

## JACK FROST

When feathery shapes appear on
windows, and the landscape is white and
sparkling, children are told that Jack Frost
has been at work with his paintbrush. Jack
first appeared in Norse lore as Jokul Frosti
(meaning "icicle frost"), son of the
wind god Kari. In Europe and
North America, he is usually
shown as a mischievous elf.

# Blowing in the wind

Air is restless and moves all the time. When it moves quickly enough for you to feel it on your face, it is called wind. Some winds blow all by themselves in one place—others are part of a big, wavy pattern that covers Earth.

## Magic winds
Bands of high winds called jet streams go around Earth from west to east. They are so strong that pilots can cut hours off their flight times if they fly along with them.

*Wispy clouds caught in the jet stream over north Africa.*

## Spinning air
When clouds get caught up in wind, their graceful patterns reflect the swooping, swirling way air sometimes moves.

*Wind is just moving air.*

## Powerful force
It takes strong, steady winds to make a tree grow like this. The winds don't actually bend the trunk, though. They kill all the shoots, buds, and leaves on the side that faces the winds, so only the protected side can grow.

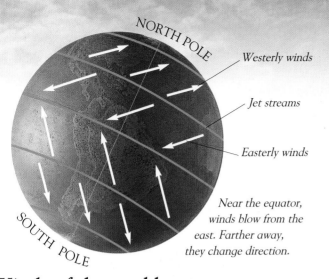

NORTH POLE

Westerly winds

Jet streams

Easterly winds

SOUTH POLE

*Near the equator, winds blow from the east. Farther away, they change direction.*

## Blown away

When desert sand is blown around by fierce winds, it can wear away solid rock. This leaves weird shapes that look like modern sculpture.

## Winds of the world

The Sun's heat and the way Earth turns create wind patterns. These are so reliable that sailors used them for centuries to cross the oceans.

*Many sand sculptures are top-heavy because wind tends to wear away the rock near the ground.*

The lightest winds are called *breezes*— the strongest are *gales.*

## Windy facts

• When a cold wind is blowing, the temperature feels much lower than it really is. This effect is called the wind-chill factor.

• Wind is measured according to the Beaufort scale, first developed for use at sea. This scale has 13 points: Force 0 is calm and Force 12 is a hurricane.

# Electric skies

Lightning bolts are huge electrical charges created when the ice and water inside storm clouds rub together. More than 3 million of them flash across the skies every day.

*Lightning moves at a speed of 23,000 miles per second (37,000 km per second).*

## Lightning facts

- Thunder is the noise lightning makes, but we don't hear it right away because light travels faster than sound.

- One fork of lightning carries enough electricity to light a whole town for a year.

- The names of two of Santa's reindeer, Donner and Blitzen, are the German words for thunder and lightning.

## Chosen paths
Lightning can flash
– inside a single cloud
– between a cloud and the air nearby
– between two clouds
– between a cloud and the ground below

*When lightning flashes, it makes the air five times as hot as the Sun's surface.*

*Lightning bolts can be up to 4 miles (6 km) long.*

## Danger!

Never shelter from a storm underneath a tree, since lightning is attracted to anything that stands high above the ground.

## Direct hit

Although a lightning bolt lasts only a fraction of a second, its heat is so intense that it can set fire to a building or a tree.

27

# Terrible twisters

Tornadoes are terrifying funnels of spinning air. They contain super-fast winds with deadly power to smash houses, flip cars over, and knock trains off their tracks.

## Birth of a monster

Tornadoes begin as warm air drawn into the base of huge storm clouds. Warm air is lighter than cool air, so it rises quickly. Then, like water flowing into a drain, it starts to spin down. If it spins fast enough, it touches the ground in the form of a deadly funnel.

Tornado warning!

## Tornado facts

● At the center of a big tornado, the wind can reach 250 mph (400 km/h).

● A tornado can flatten one house, and leave the one next door standing.

● During a 16-hour period in April 1974, 148 twisters hit "Tornado Alley" in the central US, killing 315 people and injuring 5,484 more.

## Tornado Alley

There are more tornadoes in the central United States than anywhere else on Earth. In the area where they are most common—nicknamed "Tornado Alley"—most houses have a storm cellar or basement where the family can take cover if a tornado is on the way.

*Radar devices like this one can detect signs of a tornado developing inside a storm cloud.*

## Tracking the twisters

Because they destroy any instruments in their path, tornadoes are hard to study. Special radar dishes mounted on the backs of huge trucks help to work out where they are going.

## Death and destruction

Tornadoes destroy property, nature, and human life, all within minutes. Here, a quiet town in the state of Georgia has been torn apart.

*This tangle of crushed metal was once a large, heavy truck.*

# Deadly storms

Hurricanes are the most violent and devastating storms on Earth. They almost always start in tropical places. In different parts of the world, hurricanes are also known as typhoons and cyclones.

*Photographed from space, Hurricane Fran moves across the Caribbean Sea toward Florida in 1996.*

*At the center of every tropical storm is a small patch of calm called the eye. The strongest and deadliest winds of all spin around the eye of the storm.*

## Monsters from the sea

Hurricanes get their power from the heat of tropical seas and the fact that Earth turns fastest near the equator. They start as small storms, then build into swirling clouds of wind and rain.

## Lethal water

Hurricanes whip up high, pounding waves. These cause huge damage along nearby coasts and for some distance inland.

## Stormy facts

● Hurricanes are graded from 1 to 5. Number 1 is a storm that can cause slight damage, while 5 means a potential disaster.

● Since the 1940s, hurricanes have been given human names. At first they were girls' names only, but since the 1970s, boys' names have been used one year, and girls' names the next.

## Run for cover!

When scientists expect a huge storm, they advise people to leave nearby towns and cities. Here, residents of Florida head for safety before Hurricane Andrew hit in 1992.

## Fatal wind

When Andrew did reach land (known as "making landfall"), it flattened everything in its path. In total, it killed 65 people and destroyed more than 25,000 homes.

# Tricks of the light

Every day, the Sun puts on light shows far more
dramatic than anything technology has to offer.
As well as multicolored rainbows, it can create
magical icebows, shimmering auroras,
and glowing spots in the sky.

*Ancient legends describe a pot of gold at the end of every rainbow.*

### Magic drops

Rainbow colors always
appear in the same order. Red
is at the top, then orange, yellow,
green, blue, and indigo, with violet
at the bottom. The bigger the
rainbow, the brighter and
sharper the colors will be.

## MAGIC DROPS

Light is made up of seven colors. These are the colors we see in a
rainbow. When the Sun shines through raindrops, its light bends
and reflects off their surface. The different colors
bend at different angles, though. This
separates them
into the layered
bands of light
we call a
rainbow.

## Dazzling displays

Often called "northern lights" or "southern lights" because they appear at the north and south poles, auroras are vast sheets of green streaked with pink and blue. They are caused by electrical storms on the Sun.

## Mock moon

If ice crystals fall through the atmosphere at night, they produce a sundog-like effect beside the moon. These spots are called moondogs.

## Second Sun

Falling ice crystals are able to bend the Sun's rays like raindrops do. This creates large bright spots that look almost like another Sun. Such spots are called sundogs.

## Frozen light

At the poles, the air is always freezing, so clouds are made of tiny ice crystals instead of water vapor. Inside these crystals, light has no room to separate into colors, so icebows look white.

## Watery facts

● One side of a ship is always windier than the other. This is called the windward side; the sheltered side is the lee.

● When seawater freezes into ice, it's not salty any more—all the salt is left in the surrounding water.

# Out at sea

The ingredients that make up our weather—like temperature, water, and wind—work in the same way at sea as they do on dry land. But the end results are often very different.

## Winds and waves

The winds that blow over our oceans are really strong because there are no large obstacles to slow them down. These powerful winds push the seawater into waves. During big storms, huge waves can reach the top of a lighthouse.

## Iced water

Icebergs are huge chunks of ice that have broken off glaciers at the north and south poles. Here, the seas are so cold that icebergs can stay frozen for hundreds of years.

You can only see the tip of an iceberg—most of it is underwater.

*Centuries ago, sailors thought waterspouts were blown by huge sea monsters.*

## Waterspouts

When they form at sea, whirlwinds and tornadoes are called waterspouts. The biggest ones can suck up so much water that ships in the area get sucked up, too.

## Fog banks

If warm, moist air blows over cold seas, thick fog forms in high mounds called banks. This fog is very dangerous for sailors, since they can't tell where they're going or what's in front of them.

# Desert worlds

Rainy days may make you miserable, but people who live in desert regions would give anything to get wet. Deserts—which can be cold as well as hot—are places where there is almost no rain at all.

## Green islands

An island of greenery called an oasis sometimes springs up in the middle of a desert. This happens when underground springs seep up to the surface, making it possible for plants to grow.

*Desert travelers often think they see water in the distance when there is really only sand.*

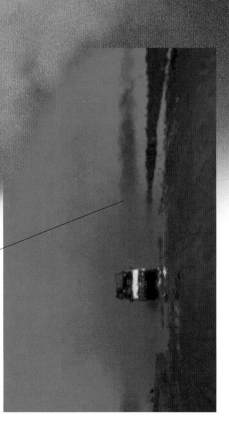

## Seeing things

Heat rising up from the ground can make light shimmer so it looks like shallow water. This false image is called a mirage.

## Desert facts

● The driest place on Earth is the Atacama Desert in Chile, where it only rains about once every six years.

● Some deserts are covered with sand dunes. These move constantly in the wind, so no plants can take hold. Even borders between countries can't be marked clearly.

## Dry storms

A lot of desert land is made of sand instead of soil. When the wind blows hard, it creates swirling clouds of choking, blinding sand and dust. At their worst, sandstorms cause more damage than the thickest blizzards.

## Whirling clouds

When desert ground gets hot, the air above it can swirl upward to form spirals as high as 350 ft (100 m). If dust or sand is sucked into these whirlwinds, they're known as dust devils or sand devils. Australians call them "willy-willies."

## Thirsty stems

Desert plants are specially adapted for dry weather. Cacti, for example, are thick and fleshy so they can keep moisture inside them for a very long time.

# Weird weather

No matter how much we learn about the weather, it can still come up with a few surprises. Have you ever seen a mud shower, an ice storm, or a black sky in the afternoon?

## Blankets of black

As volcanic clouds spread, they block out the Sun. This dark sky hung over the Philippines in 1991, when Mount Pinatubo erupted, covering everything in gray ash.

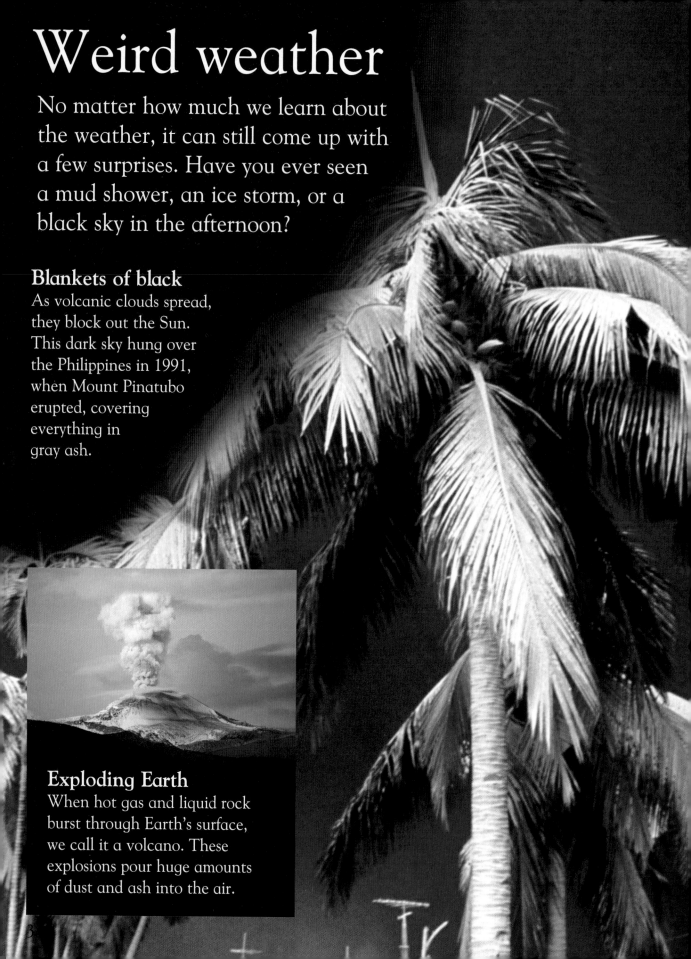

## Exploding Earth

When hot gas and liquid rock burst through Earth's surface, we call it a volcano. These explosions pour huge amounts of dust and ash into the air.

## It's raining mud

When dust storms (or volcanic dust and ash) get mixed up with rain, the result is falling mud. This messy shower is another result of Mount Pinatubo's 1991 eruption.

## Mischievous boy

Every few years, a warm ocean current appears off South America. Known as "El Niño" (the Boy Child) because it comes at Christmas, this current upsets weather systems all over the world.

## Angry ocean

El Niño warms the seas off California. This causes violent storms along the coast and as far inland as Nevada, two hundred miles away.

## Ice storms

Rain that falls through freezing air forms a layer of clear ice when it lands. This coating or glaze can be heavy enough to bring down telephone and electricity poles. When these lines came down in Oklahoma, thousands of families lost their power.

# Weather forecasting

Nobody wants to have a picnic in the rain, or go to the seashore when it's cloudy and cold. To help us make plans, we depend on weather forecasts. Daily forecasts are quite accurate, but figuring out what the weather will do over weeks and months is much harder.

### Up, up, and away
Watched by curious penguins, this scientist is releasing a weather balloon over Antarctica. The instruments attached to it measure temperature, wind, and moisture, and radio the results back to Earth.

## Ground stations

All over the world—on land, as shown here, and in the middle of the sea—weather stations gather information. This is then passed on to scientists in individual countries so they can forecast their weather.

*This weather station is located in the state of Idaho.*

## Spy satellites

Hundreds of weather satellites orbit Earth, recording pictures and data. Some move at the same speed as Earth turns, so they stay above one spot. Others fly around the planet from pole to pole.

*The first weather satellites were launched in the late 1950s.*

## View from space

Shown as a bright green swirl on this satellite image, a hurricane hits the Gulf coast of the United States.

## Weather wizardry

Huge supercomputers take in weather data from all available sources. This is fed into a model of our atmosphere so the computer can work out what effect it will have on the weather.

# Changing climates

The world's weather changes naturally over time. But experts are afraid that pollution is damaging our atmosphere and altering our climates in a bad way.

### Poison in the air

These Italian children wear protective clothes to protest against traffic pollution. Scientists think toxic gases from cars and factories trap too much heat in the atmosphere. Because they act like glass in a greenhouse, they are called "greenhouse gases." The process is known as "global warming."

Burning coal creates pollution.

Pollution leads to global warming.

### Black power

Along with exhaust fumes from cars, trucks, and buses, a main source of air pollution is smoke. Fossil fuels (like coal) create the most smoke when they are burned to produce electricity.

## Rising water

When the temperature rises by even a little, polar ice caps start to melt and affect our oceans. Scientists are afraid that if too much ice disappears, polar bears will lose much of their hunting ground.

*The light blue on this globe is the ozone layer. The big dark hole over Antarctica has been caused by pollution.*

There are holes in the ozone layer at both north and south poles.

## Dangerous exposure

As well as warming the air, pollution damages the layer of ozone that surrounds Earth. Ozone is a bluish gas that helps to block out the Sun's ultraviolet rays.

## Protect our planet

When we recycle household waste like paper and bottles, we don't need to burn so much fossil fuel to make more.

## Warming facts

● We could reduce global warming if we made better use of energy from sunlight, wind, and waves (see next page).

● Buying smaller cars—and walking when we can—will also help us to reduce greenhouse gases because we won't create so many exhaust fumes.

# Harnessing weather

Whether it feels like a friend or an enemy, weather is something we usually can't control. But today's scientists are learning how to convert its awesome power into cheap, clean energy.

## Ancient knowledge

For centuries, wind has carried balloons and kites through the air, and pushed sailing ships across lakes and seas.

*Passengers and equipment travel in a small basket suspended from the hot-air balloon.*

### Powerful facts

- Electricity generated by water—waves, tides, or waterfalls—is known as hydroelectric power.

- The biggest solar power station in the world is in the Mojave Desert in California.

- A large area of land covered with wind turbines is called a wind farm.

Solar power stations need to be built in sunny places.

## Catching the Sun

On solar power stations, huge mirrors concentrate the Sun's rays. For now, though, this technology produces quite a small amount of energy.

## Puffs of wind

These tall turbines are modern windmills that create energy. But like solar power, wind power can produce only a small amount—it takes about 3,000 turbines to equal the output of one coal power station.

## Wave power

Remote areas like the Scottish island of Islay often have no power stations. Here, harnessing the force of crashing waves is a good way to produce energy.

*Machinery designed to harness waves has to withstand the roughest seas.*

# Glossary

Here are the meanings of some words that are useful to know when you're learning about the weather.

**Acid rain** rain that has been poisoned by pollution.

**Atmosphere** the wide, layered band of air that stretches between Earth and outer space.

**Aurora** bands of colored light that appear in the sky over the north and south poles.

**Blizzard** a storm in which thick snow falls fast and hard.

**Cloud** a mass of water droplets or ice crystals in the sky.

**Condensation** what happens when water vapor in the air turns to liquid.

**Current** a ribbon of moving water in an ocean.

**Desert** a dry region that gets very little rain.

**Dew** drops of moisture that condense near the ground after a cool night.

**Equator** an imaginary line around the middle of the Earth, between the two poles.

**Evaporation** what happens when liquid disappears into the air to become water vapor.

**Fog** a cloud that is sitting on the ground. Fine fog is called mist; fog mixed with smoke is called smog.

## Golden glow

The sky sometimes turns deep red or gold when clouds of dust float up into the atmosphere. The old rhyme below suggests that a fiery sunset means fine weather the next morning, while a fiery dawn means storms are on the way.

*Red sky at night, sailors' delight;*

**Freezing** what happens when water turns into solid ice at 32°F/0°C.

**Frost** ice crystals that form when moisture in the air freezes.

**Global warming** the gradual increase in temperature of climates around the world.

**Hail** pellets of ice that fall to the ground from storm clouds.

**Hurricane** a powerful storm that brews up over tropical oceans. In different parts of the world, hurricanes are called typhoons and cyclones.

**Ice** water that gets so cold it is frozen solid.

**Lightning** a flash of static electricity in the sky.

**Precipitation** moisture released from the air onto Earth's surface. Rain, snow, hail, fog, and dew are all forms of precipitation.

**Pollution** any substance that makes air, soil, or water dirty or poisonous.

**Rain** drops of condensed water that fall from a cloud. Small, fine droplets of rain are known as drizzle.

**Rainbow** bands of colored light that form when raindrops reflect the Sun.

**Snow** clusters of ice crystals that freeze directly from vapor, without turning into drops first. Ice crystals stick together to form snowflakes before they fall.

**Tornado** a spiral of air whirling upward at very high speed.

**Troposphere** the layer of Earth's atmosphere directly above the ground. All weather takes place in the troposphere.

**Wind** the movement of air from one place to another.

ed sky in the morning, sailors take warning.

# Index

## Acknowledgments

**Dorling Kindersley would like to thank:**
Janet Allis for her original Jack Frost illustration; Laura Roberts for her help with the main Season's artwork; Fleur Star for her general editorial and research assistance, and Penny Arlon for proofreading.

## Picture credits

The publisher would like to thank the following for their kind permission to reproduce their photographs:
(Key: a=above; c=center; b=below; l=left; r=right; t=top)

Alamy Images: Brand X Pictures 6-7; Bryan & Cherry Alexander Photography 19br, Steve Bloom Images 4-5a; Cameron Davidson 31b; EuroStyle Graphics 12bl; Dennis Hallinan 14-15; Image State 3r, 21; Hans-Peter Moehlig 12tl; Plainpicture 43br; A. T. Willett 21br, 26-27b, 19trb; Jim Zuckerman 28. Ardea London Ltd: Eric Dragesco 19cl; Steve Hopkin 22bl. Bruce Coleman Ltd: 11tr. Corbis: 8t, 10-11; Phil Banko 36tl; Tom Bean 25tr; Gary W. Carter 22c; 1996 Corbis/Original image courtesy of NASA 24tl, 24cr; Rick Doyle 34-35; Frank Lane Picture Agency 20tl, 41tl; Raymond Gehman 15bl; William Manning 8-9; John M. Roberts 5bra; Galen Rowell 13br; Scott T. Smith 23; Ray Soto 35tr; Stocktrek 41cr; Hans Strand 43tr; Sygma 29cr; Craig Tuttle 22tl;

Martin B. Withers; Michael S. Yamashita 18. FLPA - Images of nature: C. Carrolho 33b; Tom & Pam Gardner 36bc. Getty Images: Alejandro Balaguer 38bl; Jose Louis Banus-March 48l,r; Tom Bean 9t; Rob Casey 5br; J.P. Fruchet 24-25, 48c; Jeri Gleiter 44tl; Lester Lefkowitz 45tl; Yannick Le Gal 34l; Jens Lucking 5tr; Nadia Mackenzie 44-45; Graeme Norways 10c; Pascal Perret 16-17; Colin Raw 42-43; Ulli Seer 46-47; Erik Simonsen 26-27t; Oliver Strewe 17tl; Harald Sund 35tl; John Wilkes 16l. Masterfile UK: Allan Davey 27tr. Nature Picture Library Ltd: Grant Mcdowell 37bl; Anup Shah 1. NASA: 6tr, 6bl, 7tr, 7br. N.H.P.A.: Ant Photo Library 36-37. Oxford Scientific Films: 39cl; Weatherstock 29tl. Pa Photos: 17r. The Palm Beach Post/Greg Lovett: C J Walker 31c. Jeff Piotrowski/Storm Productions: 29br. Planetary Visions: 41b. Popperfoto: 15cr. Powerstock: Walter Bibikow 32; Fabio Muzzi 15t; Stock Image 10bl. Reuters: 29bl. Rex Features: Sipa Press 38-39, 39tl; Son 27br. Science Photo Library: 18tlb; Martin Bond 45cr; Alan L. Detrick 5cr; David Ducros 4-5b; Jack Finch 33tr; Simon Fraser 11tl; R.B.Husar /NASA 39cr; Ted Kinsman 19tcb, 19tl; NASA 30, 43c; Stephen J. Krasemann 33c; Pekka Parviainen 12-13, 22br; Claude Nuridsany & Marie Perennou 2tc, 18tl, 18tlbr, 19tl, 19tc, 19tr; George Post 20-21; Jim Reed 20l, 21tr, 41br; Francoise Sauze 13tr; David Vaughan 33cl. Still Pictures: 39br; Denis Bringard 5trb; Angelo Doto 42l; Roland Seitre 40-41.

All other images © Dorling Kindersley www.dkimages.com